ANCIENT ROME

BY CHARLIE SAMUELS

W
FRANKLIN WATTS
LONDON•SYDNEY

First published in Great Britain in 2015 by
The Watts Publishing Group

Copyright © 2015 Brown Bear Books Ltd

For Brown Bear Books Ltd:
Editorial Director: Lindsey Lowe
Managing Editor: Tim Cooke
Children's Publisher: Anne O'Daly
Art Director: Jeni Child
Designer: Lynne Lennon
Picture Manager: Sophie Mortimer

Dewey no. 937

ISBN: 978 1 4451 4264 7

Printed in China

Franklin Watts
An imprint of
Hachette Children's Group
Part of the Watts Publishing Group
Carmelite House
50 Victoria Embankment
London EC4Y 0DZ

An Hachette UK company
www.hachette.co.uk

www.franklinwatts.co.uk

CONTENTS

INTRODUCTION

There are signs of the ancient Romans everywhere in their former empire: walls and bridges, spectacular aqueducts, villas and the famous straight paved roads. The Romans were great builders, but construction was only one aspect of technology at work in the Roman Empire. Technology also shaped, for example, farming and food production, the production of textiles and the creation of spectacular glassware. Many Roman 'inventions' were actually adopted from earlier

At a time when most buildings were wooden, cities built of stone were a demonstration of the power of the Roman Empire.

Roman homes were heated by hypocausts. These spaces under the floors were filled with hot air from a furnace, which heated the floors above.

peoples, such as the Greeks. Technology often changed in a series of tiny improvements, rather than in great steps.

RISE AND FALL OF ROME

Rome began its rise to power after its citizens declared a republic in 509 BCE. Over the next 300 years they came to dominate the whole Italian peninsula and parts of modern Spain. Another 300 years of warfare brought virtually the whole Mediterranean under Roman rule. After Augustus declared himself emperor in 27 BCE, the Roman Empire extended across much of Europe until 476 CE, when Rome's western territory in Europe fell to the Visigoths. This book will introduce you to the most important examples of the technology behind this remarkable period of power.

TECHNOLOGICAL BACKGROUND

The Romans did not invent their technology from scratch. They were great inventors, but they were also great copiers who adopted ideas from other peoples. The Romans owed much to their predecessors in central Italy, the Etruscans, and to the ancient Greeks who had earlier dominated the eastern Mediterranean and colonised parts of southern Italy.

This arch in the Italian city of Volterra was built by the Etruscans, the original rulers of the town of Rome.

Roman ships were based on the vessels the ancient Greeks had used to trade in the eastern Mediterranean.

The Etruscans built large cities with roads, sewers and water systems. They used aqueducts to bring fresh water to their cities. They also developed metalworking, the use of metals. Their public buildings used the arch and the vault. The Romans would use and improve on all these techniques.

THE GREEK LEGACY

From the Greeks, the Romans took a love of culture, such as art, music and poetry. But the Romans also used Greek ideas about architecture. Their shipping was based on Greek vessels. They used everyday Greek technology, such as minting coins and making glass. However, some Greek science, particularly mathematics, was too sophisticated for the Romans. It fell into disuse and was only revived later.

BUILDING

Many Roman structures still stand around 2,000 years after they were built. Roman builders understood the forces that supported walls and roofs. Roman leaders commissioned impressive buildings made from stone and concrete to demonstrate the strength and power of the empire.

Building a Basilica

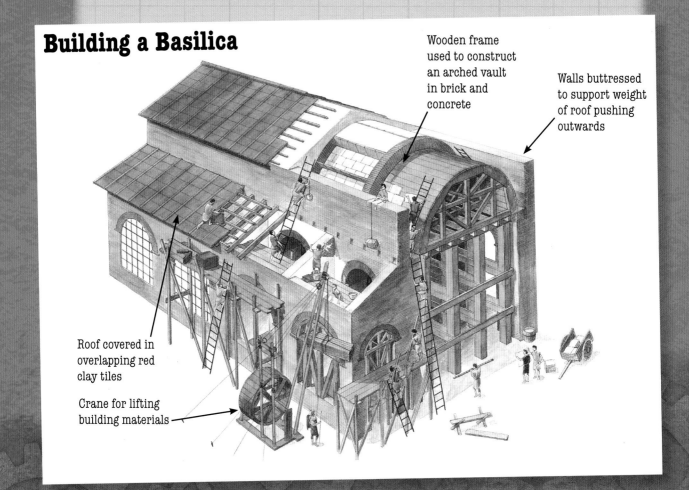

Wooden frame used to construct an arched vault in brick and concrete

Walls buttressed to support weight of roof pushing outwards

Roof covered in overlapping red clay tiles

Crane for lifting building materials

HOW TO...

The Greeks and the Etruscans had used arches in building, but the Romans perfected the stone arch. An arch uses sideways forces to hold downward weight. Once its keystone is in place, it becomes very strong. Roman builders used arches to build strong but light aqueducts, bridges and arenas.

Keystone

Wooden frame supports structure during construction

The Romans built cities across Europe. They constructed large public buildings for government use and temples for worship. They built luxury villas for the wealthy and tall blocks of flats for the poor. They were expert water engineers – every city had a public baths. Aqueducts brought clean water to towns and drains took sewage away.

THE CITY OF ROME

At the heart of the empire was Rome itself. It contained the best examples of Roman architecture, such as the Colosseum, and the Pantheon. To undertake such big building projects needed the huge numbers of slaves owned throughout the Roman Empire.

TECHNICAL SPECS

- The Romans developed the use of concrete for building; they mixed a volcanic ash called pozzolana with rubble to produce a light but strong material.
- Concrete made it possible for the ancient Romans to invent the dome. The massive dome of the Pantheon in Rome remains the largest of its type in the world.
- The Romans fired clay to make bricks. Mobile high-temperature kilns allowed bricks to be introduced right across the Roman Empire.
- The Romans used small squares of coloured glass to create elaborate decorations – mosaics – for the floors of large villas and important public buildings.

THE PANTHEON

Few Roman buildings exist in their original form. The Pantheon in Rome is the most spectacular. It was built for Emperor Hadrian between 118 and 125 CE. It used the most advanced building techniques of the time. This was fitting for a structure that was probably intended to honour all the Roman gods.

The recesses inside the dome helped to reduce its weight and also let the concrete in the dome dry more quickly.

The Pantheon is a rotunda, or drum shape, topped by a dome. The interior is based on a sphere: the rotunda is 43 metres (142 ft) across; the top of the dome is the same height above the floor.

ENGINEERING MARVEL

The dome is the largest example anywhere of an unreinforced concrete dome. It was designed to be as light as possible. It is 6.4 metres (21 ft) thick at the bottom but 1.2 metres (3 ft 9 in) thick at the top. The builders used basalt to make the concrete at the base of the dome but at the top used pumice stone, which is a much lighter material.

TECHNICAL SPECS

- To support the building, its foundation walls are 7.3 metres (24 ft) thick and sink 4.5 metres (14 ft 9 in) into the ground.
- The dome was such a feat of engineering that the Pantheon is the best-preserved of all ancient Roman buildings.
- A ring of brick arches around the top of the rotunda walls helps to support the weight of the dome.
- The concrete of the dome is full of hidden hollows to reduce its weight.
- The building materials and techniques used to lighten the weight of the dome reduced the stresses acting on it by as much as 80 per cent.

Inside the Pantheon

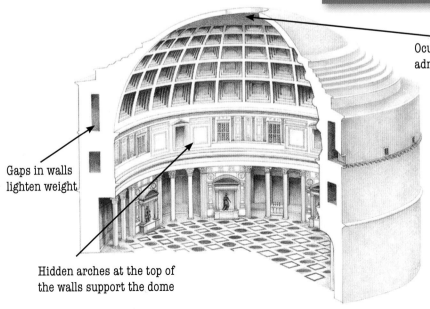

Oculus, hole to admit light

Gaps in walls lighten weight

Hidden arches at the top of the walls support the dome

VILLAS

Roman Villa

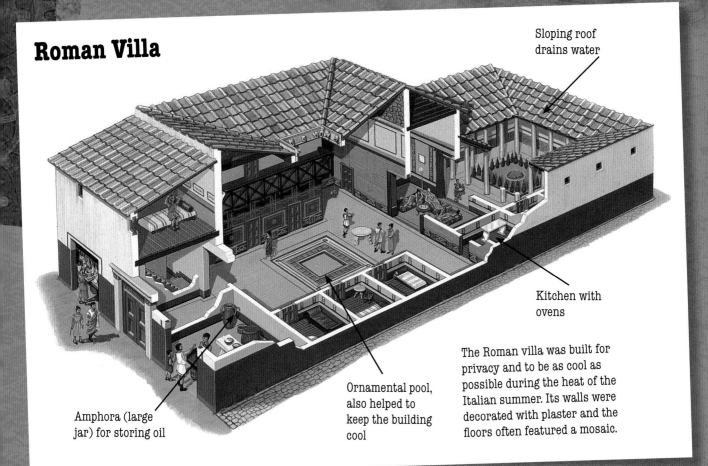

Sloping roof drains water

Kitchen with ovens

The Roman villa was built for privacy and to be as cool as possible during the heat of the Italian summer. Its walls were decorated with plaster and the floors often featured a mosaic.

Ornamental pool, also helped to keep the building cool

Amphora (large jar) for storing oil

Technology enabled wealthy Romans to build comfortable country villas to provide an escape from city life. The villas were designed for privacy. At their centre an open atrium, or hall, often with a small pond, kept the building cool in summer. There were very few windows, which was another way of keeping out heat.

Roman villas had kitchens with brick-lined ovens, rooms for bathing and even a lavatory. Roman ovens burned wood or charcoal. Slaves also kept a furnace burning. It heated water for bathing and also supplied heating to at least one room. Hot air from the furnace passed through a hypocaust made up of underfloor passages, before escaping through flues in the walls.

COMMUNAL LAVATORIES

The lavatory was not a private space, as it is now. It had a row of seats that were used by more than one person at a time. Running water flushed away the sewage.

TECHNICAL SPECS

- Villas were built of brick covered with plaster; the Romans perfected the mass production of clay bricks.
- Roofs used two types of red tiles: flat *tegulae* covered the surface; the vertical joins between tegulae were covered by semicircular *imbrexes*.
- Roman homes were designed to make the most of the natural light.
- Roofs slanted down over the atrium; this allowed rainwater to collect in the central pool.
- In the countryside, villas used rain-water or rivers for water; in the town, running water came into the home via pipes.

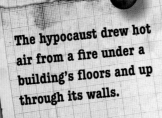

The hypocaust drew hot air from a fire under a building's floors and up through its walls.

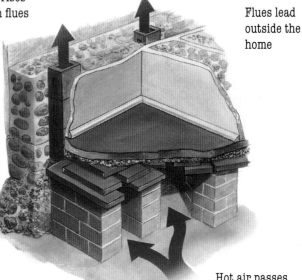

Hot air rises through flues

Flues lead outside the home

Hot air passes beneath the floor

THE COLOSSEUM

The Colosseum in Rome was a triumph of engineering. It held 50,000 spectators to watch events such as gladiatorial contests. It was built in just eight years, from 72 to 80 CE, and was named the Flavian Amphitheatre after the family name of the emperors who built it, Vespasian and Titus.

The arena no longer has its floor, so the ruins of the *hypogeum*, or basement, are clearly visible.

↑

The walls of the Colosseum used a series of arches to support the weight of the spectators seated inside.

ADAPTABLE ARENA

The Colosseum staged shows from gladiatorial fights to mock sea battles, for which the arena was flooded with water. No-one knows how this was done. Water may have been brought in huge wooden containers from an aqueduct. The arena was filled with 4 million litres of water; sluice gates were opened to drain it.

Emperor Domitian added a basement level, the hypogeum. These underground tunnels held wild animals and gladiators in 32 cages. They were winched up into the arena by mechanical lifts.

TECHNICAL SPECS

- It would have taken seven hours to fill the Colosseum with water to a depth of 1.5 metres (5 ft).
- The shape of the Colosseum was an ellipse (oval), not a circle, in order to give as many people as possible a good view of the arena.
- During the Roman summer, shade was provided by a series of awnings at the top of the structures, supported by 240 wooden masts and a system of ropes and stays.
- Seating reflected social position. The senators and rich people sat in the front rows.
- Arched vaults on the ground floor provided separate entrances numbered from 1 to 80.

HADRIAN'S WALL

The wall followed natural features, such as these crags. In the foreground are the ruins of a milecastle.

One of the most remarkable examples of Roman engineering was built to defend the border of the Roman empire from peoples in what is now Scotland. Hadrian's Wall was built by Emperor Hadrian in northern Britain between 122 and 128 CE. It joined the east and west coasts: a distance of 80 Roman miles (117 kilometres/72 miles).

Large sections of the wall survive intact, proving the high quality of the original building. The wall was built by soldiers from three Roman legions and used natural features, such as crags, to make it virtually impregnable. Building the wall took six years in the harsh climate of northern Britain; it was later enhanced with the addition of larger forts.

GUARDING THE BORDER

Gates were set into the wall at regular intervals. They allowed people to pass through in order to trade, if they were unarmed. There were turrets every 495 metres (540 yards), milecastles every Roman mile and forts every 11 kilometres (7 miles). About 11,500 soldiers manned the wall until the fall of the Roman Empire in the fifth century.

TECHNICAL SPECS

- The plan was for a wall 3.3 metres (10 ft) wide and 4 metres (12 ft) tall; much of the finished wall was lower and narrower, although in places it reached a height of nearly 6 metres (20 ft).
- The wall was built of rubble and concrete finished with limestone.
- The width of the wall varies along its length.
- The walls had ditches on either side. The *vallum* – the broader ditch – lay behind the wall.
- Because the wall followed the landscape's natural contours, it was rarely straight.
- A series of 80 milecastles stand at intervals of approximately 1 Roman mile along its length.

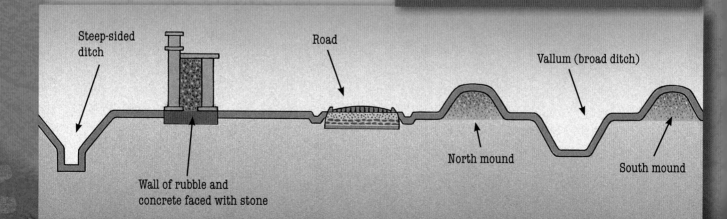

Steep-sided ditch

Road

Vallum (broad ditch)

North mound

South mound

Wall of rubble and concrete faced with stone

AQUEDUCTS

The Pont du Gard was built in Gaul – now southern France – by Emperor Trajan in the first century CE.

Aqueducts were systems of channels and pipes that brought water into Roman cities. They allowed homes to have running water, indoor plumbing and a sewerage system. Eleven separate aqueducts carried water into Rome. Within the city, the water was stored in huge cisterns and fed into houses through a series of lead pipes.

The Romans borrowed the idea of aqueducts from the Etruscans and Greeks. But the Roman system marked a leap forward in water management. Some 800 kilometres (500 miles) of aqueducts fed the city of Rome itself.

GRADIENTS AND ARCHES

Aqueducts worked by using a gentle downwards gradient and gravity to carry water from springs and lakes. Most were underground conduits, which kept the water cool and clean. Where it was too difficult to dig, however, aqueducts ran above ground. When the path crossed a valley, the Romans sometimes built a bridge of levels of arches, with the water channel at the top level.

TECHNICAL SPECS

- Aqueducts were built from a combination of stone, brick and waterproof cement.
- Underground channels were made from stone and terracotta pipes.
- Most aqueducts were less than 1 metre (3 ft) underground, so they were easy to maintain.
- The Aqua Claudia carried water from two springs 70 kilometres (44 miles) into Rome.
- The Pont du Gard in France had a gentle gradient; it dropped only 17 metres (56 ft) vertically in its 50-kilometre (30-mile) length.

Aqueducts were built in layers. The top level carried water; a lower level sometimes carried a road.

ROMAN BATHS

The Romans were careful about keeping clean, but few homes had private baths. Instead, Romans used the *thermae*, or public baths. These baths were more than places to get clean; they were public spaces where people met and relaxed. Usually set out around a garden, the baths were carefully engineered.

The Roman baths at Bath in England were built on a hot spring. The buildings were updated in the early 18th century by the Georgians.

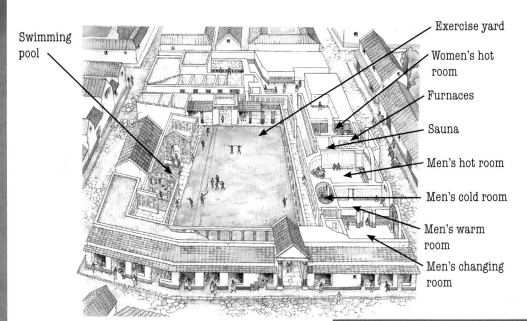

Swimming pool

Exercise yard

Women's hot room

Furnaces

Sauna

Men's hot room

Men's cold room

Men's warm room

Men's changing room

The Baths at Pompeii

Once they were undressed, bathers entered a *caldarium* (hot bathroom). Soap was very expensive, so most bathers covered themselves in olive oil. They scraped the oil and dirt off their skin with curved metal tools called strigils. They then passed through a *tepidarium* (warm room) before plunging into a *frigidarium* (cold bathroom).

HEATED WATER

Fresh water was fed into the baths through pipes from the nearest cistern. For the warm and hot baths, water was heated in boilers. Some baths also used hypocausts to create steam rooms.

TECHNICAL SPECS

- Some baths used water from natural hot springs, which was diverted by pipes into the buildings; they included the famous baths at Aqua Sulis in Bath, England.
- Slaves kept furnaces burning to keep the air hot or warm.
- Where there were no hot springs, boilers were used to store water; the caldarium boiler was closest to the fire, the tepidarium boiler further away and the frigidarium boiler furthest away.
- Hot air circulated beneath the floor and in the walls of the caldarium; the floor was so hot bathers had to wear wooden clogs.

MILLING

Bread was the staple food throughout the Roman Empire. To grind grain to make flour, ancient peoples traditionally relied on animal-powered mills. But as early as the 1st century BCE, when the growing population needed more food, the Romans began using water to power mills.

The Romans worked out the best shape for a millstone, and how quickly it should rotate to be most efficient at grinding corn.

Mills at Arles

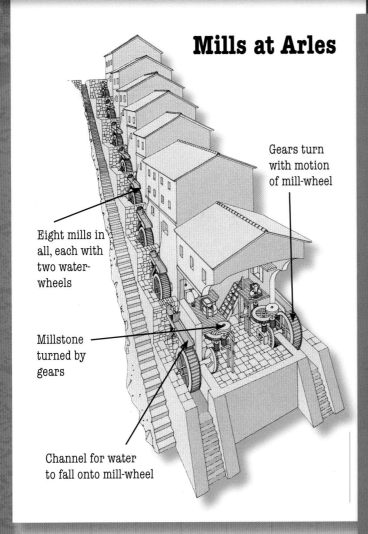

Gears turn with motion of mill-wheel

Eight mills in all, each with two water-wheels

Millstone turned by gears

Channel for water to fall onto mill-wheel

TECHNICAL SPECS

- The Romans adopted water-mills from the Greeks, but improved the technology.
- Water-mills were turned either by water flowing from the top (overshot mills) or flowing in a stream beneath the wheel (undershot mills).
- The energy of the water-wheels was transmitted by a gear mechanism to millstones.
- The Romans changed the shape of millstones, which became wider and squatter; the faces of the stone that rubbed together became smaller.
- Roman millstones were made of basalt; the rock has natural grooves and edges that helped grind the grain more finely.

A MILL COMPLEX

At Barbegal, near Arles in southern France, the Romans built the largest mill complex in the empire during the second century CE. It comprised 16 water-mills in eight pairs, running down the side of a hill from an aqueduct. The water ran from mill to mill and into a drain at the bottom of the hill. Enough flour could be milled to feed the whole population of Arles, about 12,500 people. By no longer using donkeys or horses to power mills, water-mills also freed these beasts of burden to do other jobs.

COMMUNICATIONS

Horses pulled carts and also provided a courier service that could carry messages up to 230 kilometres (145 miles) a day.

Running a vast empire depended on reliable communications. People and goods moved easily on the famous Roman network of roads or by boat. Most people walked; they could cover between 20 and 25 kilometres (12–15 miles) a day. Thanks to the good roads, a horse-drawn cart could cover up to 56 kilometres (35 miles) a day.

For shorter, cheaper journeys, slaves carried goods on their backs. Carts pulled by oxen were used in the countryside. Soldiers, politicians, traders and tourists all travelled widely. If they did not know where they were going, they used an *itinerarium*. These early maps listed places and the distances between them.

SEA TRAVEL

During the summer months ships crossed the seas laden with goods. Sailing could be dangerous, however. There were no compasses and shipwrecks were common because ships sailed close to the coast whenever possible. Pirates were no longer a threat, though, as the Romans had brought peace across the Mediterranean.

TECHNICAL SPECS

- The Romans built canals to move freight; the canal that connected Portus, at the mouth of the River Tiber, with Rome's port at Ostia was 90 metres (100 yards) wide.
- Chariots and carts had wheels with iron rims.
- *Raeda* (Roman coaches) could carry up to 1,000 Roman *libra* (327 kilograms/720 pounds) of people and luggage; they were box-shaped and were covered with a cloth roof to shelter the passengers inside.

The Romans built harbours, such as this one, for unloading ships that carried cargo across the Mediterranean.

ROAD BUILDING

From the fourth century BCE, the Romans built a network of stone roads to connect their sprawling empire. The roads were important for officials and merchants. But they were also useful for moving troops rapidly in case of trouble. The roads were so well constructed that many remain in use today.

Roman roads followed a straight line set out by surveyors using a sighting stick called a groma.

HOW TO...

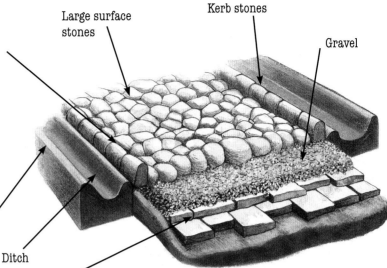

The layered structure of Roman roads gave them great stability, which is one reason why some are still in use, some 2,000 years after they were built. The surface stones allowed rain-water to drain into ditches at either side of the roadway.

Large surface stones

Kerb stones

Gravel

Bank

Ditch

Foundation of stone slabs

ALL ROADS LEAD TO ROME

The heart of the road system was Rome itself. Roads radiated out from the city towards all points of the empire. The first, the Appian Way, was built in 312 BCE. It ran south from Rome. Other important road hubs were Lyon in Gaul (France) and London in Britain.

By the height of the empire in the first century CE, Roman roads stretched across Europe, North Africa and the Middle East, from the Atlantic Ocean in the west to the Euphrates River in the east. The road system comprised 80,000 kilometres (50,000 miles) of highways.

TECHNICAL SPECS

- Roads were often built by work gangs of soldiers.
- The engineers first dug parallel drainage ditches about 12 metres (40 feet) apart.
- They cleared a trench between them as a road-bed.
- They laid a foundation of stone slabs, covered with sand or mortar. They added a layer of crushed stones.
- On top they laid stone slabs or cobbles in mortar, which allowed rain-water to drain into the drainage ditches.
- Large roads were often lined by kerb stones up to 20 centimetres (8 inches) high on either side.

SHIPBUILDING

Merchant Ship

Rome's empire relied on merchant ships, or *corbitas*. They transported wheat, wine, oil and cloth. The ships carried large wooden swans' heads that represented the Egyptian goddess Isis, the guardian of seafarers.

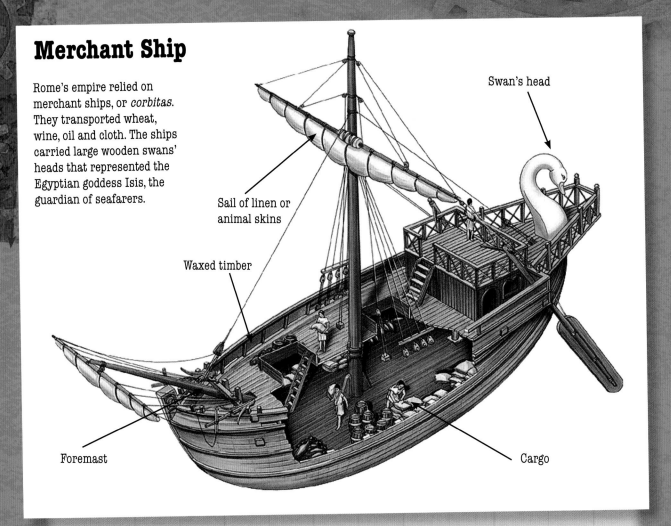

Swan's head

Sail of linen or animal skins

Waxed timber

Foremast

Cargo

Roman ships were built using Mediterranean methods that dated back to early Greece. Merchant ships carried cargo throughout a network of trade routes that covered the Roman Empire. Warships were used to enforce Rome's dominance of the Mediterranean, which the Romans called *Mare Nostrum*, 'Our Sea'.

The main cargo vessel was the *corbita*. It had a rounded hull and a curved prow and stern. The corbita was clumsy and slow, but it was very seaworthy. It sailed as far as India.

WARSHIPS

The standard Roman warship was the *quinquereme*. It may have had five rowers to each oar, and a total crew of about 300 men. The galleys were rowed at high speed into enemy ships. A ram holed the enemy ship underwater, while soldiers rushed across ramps to engage in hand-to-hand fighting.

TECHNICAL SPECS

- Shipbuilders laid the keel first then added the planks of the hull.
- The planks were joined closely edge to edge.
- The hulls were waterproofed with wax, tarred fabric or lead sheets.
- A corbita cuold carry up to 350 tonnes (385 tons).
- The largest cargo ships were grain carriers. When used for passengers, grain ships could carry 600 people.
- The average speed of a merchant ship was 3.5 knots (6.5 kmh/4 mph). A galley could be rowed at speeds of up to 12 knots (22 kmh/14 mph).

Some galleys carried a drawbridge to allow soldiers board enemy ships, but the weight made galleys unstable.

FARMING

The basis of the Roman economy was farming. The main crop was wheat: bread made from it was eaten at every meal. The Romans also grew grapes, which were made into wine, and olives to produce olive oil. Many farms were absorbed into *latifundia* (large estates). These were worked by slaves who supplied cheap labour.

A slave shepherd watches his sheep while other slaves harvest olives (left) and grapes from vines (right).

The land was prepared for crops by using oxen to pull ploughs. Early 'ard' ploughs were little more than sharp sticks. The Romans added an extra blade named a coulter, which broke up the ground in front of the ard. Crops were originally harvested by hand, using sickles. In the first century CE, a reaping machine named the *vallus* was invented.

SAVING THE SOIL

The Romans practised crop rotation and mixed farming. This allowed the soil to rest, so that it did not become too depleted of nutrients by over-use of the land.

TECHNICAL SPECS

- The Romans grew emmer, an ancient type of wheat that had twice as much protein as modern wheat.
- Wheat cultivation was labour intensive; wheat had to be cut, threshed and winnowed to separate the grain, and the grain stored; the Romans introduced machines for various stages of the task.
- Vast amounts of forest were cleared to make way for farmland.
- Grapes were pressed to make wine either by foot or by using a mechanical screw press.
- The Romans introduced olive cultivation across their empire.

Farm Machines

Mechanical Reaper (Vallus)

Blades separate ears of corn from stalks

Ploughs

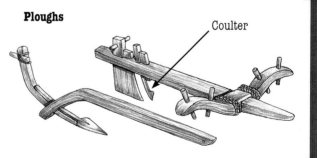

Coulter

The ard (above left) had a metal tip to turn the soil. Romans in Gaul developed a new type of plough (right). It had a coulter in front of the plough blade that could dig and turn the heavier soils of northern Europe.

MILITARY TECHNOLOGY

Armour

Roman soldiers wore flexible armour made from overlapping iron scales that were hinged at the back and fastened together at the front. The armour was held together by straps of leather. Helmets were based on Celtic designs and were made of bronze. Soldiers carried an oval shield made of wood and covered with linen and calfskin. There were iron strips on the shield to protect against sword thrusts.

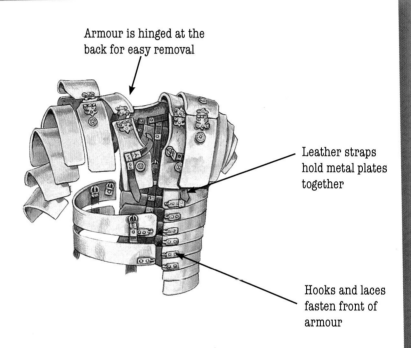

Armour is hinged at the back for easy removal

Leather straps hold metal plates together

Hooks and laces fasten front of armour

The Romans relied on military strength to conquer Italy and then to expand and maintain their empire. Roman soldiers used weapons including axes, spears, daggers and swords. They also had body armour and shields, such as the *scutum*. Larger weapons besieged enemy cities, an important part of Roman wafare.

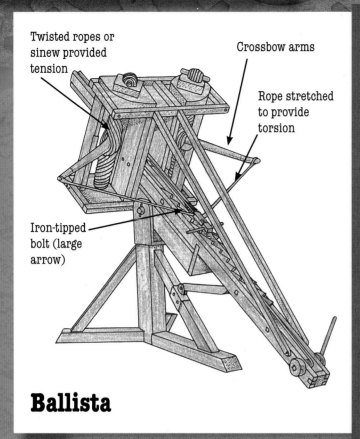

Twisted ropes or sinew provided tension

Crossbow arms

Rope stretched to provide torsion

Iron-tipped bolt (large arrow)

Ballista

Attacking Roman armies used siege engines, which they wheeled up to city walls. There were *aries* (battering rams) and *terebras* (drills) to break through defences. There were also tall wooden towers from which soldiers could climb onto the walls via a drawbridge. Other large weapons included the *ballista*, a massive crossbow that fired flaming arrows or bolts, and the *onager*, a catapult that threw stone balls up to 425 metres (1,400 feet).

PERSONAL WEAPONS

For hand-to-hand fighting, a Roman soldier was armed with a metal-covered *scutum* (shield), a *gladius* (sword), a metal-tipped *pilium* (spear), a bronze helmet and metal armour.

WEIGHTS AND MEASURES

The Roman Empire was based on trade that was often carried on at long distance between different peoples. It was important to have standard weights and measures for trade and construction throughout Roman territory. The most important unit was probably the Roman mile: it even dictated the empire's borders.

The Romans were the first to use the word mile (Latin *mille*, or 'a thousand'). It referred to a thousand paces. The mile was used to mark distances on Roman roads and to decide where to position fortifications. No-one knows exactly how long it was: it was probably nearly 1,520 metres (5,000 feet).

This vessel was used to measure a unit of volume called a *modius*; weights and measures were controlled by the empire.

SURVEYING

Among the uses of measurements was surveying. Surveyors marked out roads, fortifications and the sites of bridges and cities. They used measuring sticks and simple tools. The groma – two crossed sticks on top of a vertical staff – helped work out straight lines and right angles. This helped to work out, for example, the gradient of an aqueduct.

TECHNICAL SPECS

- The unit for weight was the unica, which was equivalent to 28 grams (1 oz); 12 unicae equalled 1 libra (336 grams/12 oz).
- The unit of dry and liquid volume was the sextarius; 1 sextarius measured around 0.55 litres (0.96 pint).
- The Roman mile was based on 1,000 paces – but the precise length of a pace is unknown.
- A Roman foot measured 29.6 centimetres (11.6 inches).
- Road distances were marked from the Milliarium Aureum ('golden milepost') in the Forum in Rome.
- Surveyors used carts equipped with toothed gear wheels to measure distances along roads; every mile, the gear wheel pushed a pebble into a container.

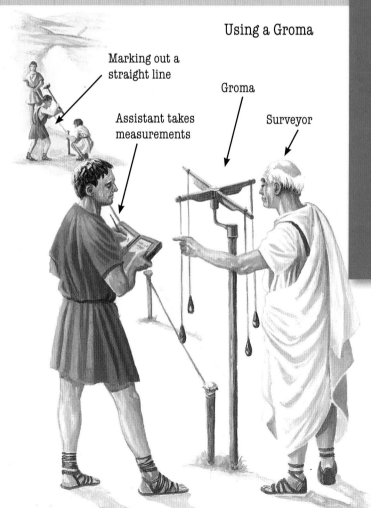

Using a Groma

Marking out a straight line

Assistant takes measurements

Groma

Surveyor

The groma had weights on its four arms to help the surveyor make sure that it was vertical.

ASTRONOMY AND THE CALENDAR

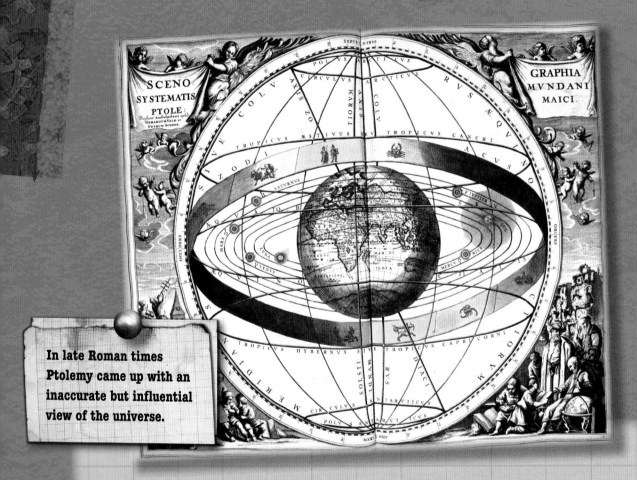

In late Roman times Ptolemy came up with an inaccurate but influential view of the universe.

The Romans made the change from a calendar based on the moon to one based on the sun. The old lunar calendar was based on the cycles of the moon. It had 12 months, and the year was 355 days long. But this lunar year was out of step with the solar year.

By the first century BCE, the calendar was out by a season. Astronomers had known for two centuries that a true year was 365.2 days long. In 46 BCE, Julius Caesar introduced a solar calendar with years of 365 days and an extra day every four years.

FAMOUS ASTRONOMER

Ptolemy was a Greek–Roman who worked in Alexandria, Egypt between 127 and 145 CE. He described a planetary system with the Earth at its centre. Ptolemy's work would influence astronomers for the next 1,400 years. It was the basis for all Roman astronomy.

The sundial arrived from Sicily in 236 BCE. The Romans used it to divide the daylight into 12 roughly equal periods – hours.

TECHNICAL SPECS

- Late in the Roman Empire, the Romans divided history at the birth of Christ: Before Christ (BC) and Anno Domini (AD), which means 'in the year of our lord.'
- Before the solar calendar could be introduced, the discrepancies that had built up from the lunar calendar needed to be ironed out, so the previous year had 445 days.
- The new calendar is known as the Julian Calendar, after Julius Caesar.
- Many of our names for months come from the Roman calendar.
- Like the Egyptians and Greeks, the Romans used sundials to tell the time of day.

TEXTILES AND DYES

Cloth-making was the largest and one of the most labour-intensive of all industries under the Romans. Everyone needed textiles for clothing, from the beautiful imported silk and cotton worn by the wealthy to the rough hemp worn by the poor. The industry included the spinning of yarn, the weaving of textiles and the use of dyes to colour the material. Like textiles, dyes varied according to wealth.

Ciampini

The Romans used an upright loom. Lead weights were tied to the end of the hanging threads.

Molluscs, such as this one, from Lebanon produced Tyrian purple; the dye was so valuable some people bought fake versions.

The most common material was wool, but linen and hemp were also widely used. Silk was imported from China and fine cotton came from India.

Preparing wool was time consuming: the fleece was immersed in water and then dried. The dry fibres were pressed, smoothed and spun on a type of spinning wheel before they were woven.

DYEING CLOTHES

Dyes came from different sources and varied widely in cost. Tyrian purple was named for Tyre in Lebanon, where it was produced from a mollusc. It was so expensive to produce that it was originally worn only by the emperor.

TECHNICAL SPECS

- Cloth was woven on vertical looms at home; poor women wove for their own families, while the wealthy used slaves to do the weaving.
- To keep clothes white, they were often washed in a solution that included urine.
- The most highly prized wool came from the sheep of Tarentum in southern Italy.
- Most dyes came from plants, and there was a relatively limited selection: saffron produced yellow, while the madder plant produced various shades of red.
- The most common source of blue dye was indigo, obtained from plants in Asia.
- Iron alum was used to stop dyes fading.

METALWORKING

Metals were important to the Romans for making tools, coins and statues. The area around Rome had few sources of metal, so metals were traded over long distances. There were mines in Italy, but the Romans imported gold and silver from Spain and Greece, tin from Britain and copper from Spain and Cyprus.

This statue of Marcus Aurelius balances on three of the horse's legs, which was a challenge for the sculptors.

This silver coin shows the two-headed god Janus; such designs were added to coins to show they were genuine.

TECHNICAL SPECS

- Mining was dangerous, so it was done by slaves who used stone or metal picks to dig out the minerals.
- The Romans used water-wheels to remove water from flooded mines.
- A cheaper substitute for gold was brass obtained by mixing copper and zinc.
- The Romans reheated iron with carbon to make a stronger metal, known as steel.
- Roman coins included the *as* (bronze), *sestertius* (a small silver coin) and *denarius* (a large silver coin). The *aureus* was a gold coin.

Metals were so scarce that metal objects were often melted down and reused. The Romans adopted coins from Greece. Roman coinage was introduced in the third century BCE. Silver coins minted in Rome were used across the empire.

MAKING STATUES

Bronze was used to cast statues. One of the most popular showed the emperor on a horse. It took great skill to cast an equestrian statue, because all the weight was supported by the horse's slender ankles. Statues of emperors were frequently melted down after the emperor died. The bronze was reused.

GLASSMAKING

The Romans adopted glassmaking from the Greeks, who used coloured glass to make vessels. For centuries, the Latin language did not even have a word for glass. That all changed in the first century CE. Suddenly glass was being used everywhere: for vases and boxes, as tiny squares in mosaics and even in windows.

The dramatic expansion in the production of glass came as a result of a new technique that had been introduced from Syria: glassblowing. Glassblowing involved heating a ball of glass until it was very soft, then blowing air through a long tube to inflate it into a hollow vessel. Glassblowing had many advantages; it was quicker than other glassmaking techniques.

This blown-glass urn was made before 300 C.E. It held the ashes of someone who had been cremated.

Vessels that were blown had thinner walls, which meant they used less glass. That in turn meant that more glass was available. Glassware went from being a high-status object to being far more common. The Romans were also recyclers: they melted down broken glass to make new vessels.

GLASS PRODUCTION

Roman glass production reached its peak in the second century CE. Different styles were produced in different parts of the Roman empire.

Glass became popular for use at the tables of rich Romans. It was easier to clean than pottery vessels, and did not taint the food as bronze vessels did.

This glass vessel shaped like a head was made in the second century in what is now the Balkans.

TECHNICAL SPECS

- In order to make glass, the Romans used a furnace to heat a mixture of silica and soda with a stabiliser (usually lime or magnesia).
- Adding specific metal oxides changed the colour of the glass.
- Cobalt was added to make dark blue glass.
- Tin was used to produce opaque white glass.
- Manganese oxide was used to make colourless glass.
- From the 1st century CE, glass *tesserae* (mosaic tiles) were manufactured; they were usually yellow, blue or green.
- Roman glass had a highly shiny surface; the examples that still survive today have not, surprisingly, become dull over the centuries.

TIMELINE

BCE

509 The Romans drive the Etruscans out of Rome; they found a republic and begin to conquer Etruscan cities.

347 Coins are introduced into Rome.

312 Roman politician Appius Claudius Caecus builds the Aqua Appia aqueduct.

300 Rome becomes the dominant power in Italy.

250 Roman farmers start using crop rotation.

241 Rome defeats Carthage in the First Punic War and takes control of Sicily.

218 Rome fights Carthage in the Second Punic War (c. 218–201)

204 Rome goes to war against Macedonia; after victory in 205, Rome dominates the western Mediterranean.

170 The world's first paved streets appear in Rome.

146 Rome establishes the province of Africa, taking control of the whole Mediterranean.

110 Romans begin using nailed horseshoes.

100 Roman builders use concrete made from crushed stones and pozzolana (volcanic ash) cement, which sets underwater.

80 Vertical undershot water-wheels are introduced in Mediterranean countries for grinding corn.

58 Julius Caesar begins a 10-year campaign to conquer Gaul (France).

46 Julius Caesar is named dictator for life in Rome. He introduces the Julian calendar.

44 Julius Caesar is assassinated in Rome.

27 Octavian becomes emperor, marking the start of the Roman Empire.

CE	
20	Pont du Gard built in France.
30	The first Latin treatise on medicine is published.
50	Aqueduct built in Segovia, Spain. Italian farmers use water-mills to grind grain.
60	Roman forces in Britain defeat Boudicca, queen of the Iceni tribe.
77	Pliny the Elder summarises Roman natural history.
79	The volcano Vesuvius erupts, burying the Roman towns of Pompeii and Herculaneum.
80	The Colosseum amphitheatre is built in Rome.
117	The Empire reaches its greatest extent under Hadrian.
128	The Pantheon is built in Rome,
150	Roman–Greek geographer Ptolemy compiles a compendium of astronomy.
286	Diocletian divides the empire into western and eastern halves.
300	The palace built for Diocletian in Split uses arches supported by free-standing columns. A mill is built near Arles in France with 16 overshot waterwheels.
312	Roman general Constantine becomes emperor after defeating imperial forces at the battle of Milvian Bridge.
330	Constantine takes the ancient city of Byzantium as his new capital, Constantinople.
350	Romans in France use a water-powered sawmill to cut marble.
410	Barbarian Visigoths, led by Alaric, sack Rome, marking the symbolic fall of the Roman Empire.
441	Attila leads the Huns in a large-scale invasion of the Roman Empire.
476	The German chieftain Odoacer deposes the last western emperor, Romulus Augustulus, marking the end of the empire in the west.

GLOSSARY

amphitheatre An oval or circular building with seating for an audience.

aqueduct A raised brick channel for carrying water.

ard A simple plough with a sharp point that turns the soil.

basalt A dark-colored type of volcanic rock.

buttressed Supported by buttresses, wood or stone supports that project from a building.

canal An artificial waterway.

cast To pour molten metal into a mould and allow it to harden.

cistern An underground tank for storing water.

concrete A strong building material made by mixing a powder such as cement with stone and water.

empire A large territory ruled by an emperor or empress.

gladiatorial Related to gladiators, who fought each other for public entertainment.

gradient The angle at which a slope descends.

hemp A plant whose fibres are used to make material.

hull The main body of a ship, including its bottom and its sides.

keel The long structure that forms the bottom of a ship and supports the whole.

kiln An oven used to harden pottery or bake bricks.

millstone A large circular stone that rubs against another stone to grind corn into flour.

mosaic A decoration made by using small pieces of coloured material to cover a surface.

rotunda A round building, usually covered with a dome.

sewerage A system of pipes to take away waste water or sewage.

siege engine A large machine used to attack the walls of a besieged city.

staple A food that makes up the major part of a diet.

strigil A curved metal rod used to scrape the skin.

surveyor Someone who carefully measures the land.

vault An arched structure that forms a ceiling or roof.

FURTHER INFORMATION

BOOKS

Brocklehurst, Ruth. *Roman Army (Usborne Discovery)*. Usborne Publishing Ltd., 2008

Dawson, Ian. *Greek and Roman Medicine* (History of Medicine). Wayland, 2005.

Hawes, Alison. *What the Romans Did For Us*. A&C Black, 2009.

Hepplewhite, Peter. *Truth or Busted: The Fact or Fiction Behind the Romans*. Wayland, 2014.

Knapman, Timothy. *History Quest: Race Through Rome*. QED Publishing, 2013.

McDonald, Fiona. *The Roman Colosseum* (Spectacular Visual Guides). Book House, 2010.

WEBSITES

http://channel.nationalgeographic.com/channel/videos/roman-tech/
National Geographic video about Roman technology in the Pantheon.

http://science.howstuffworks.com/engineering/structural/10-roman-engineering-tricks.htm
Howstuffworks page on '10 Cool Engineering Tricks the Romans Taught Us'.

http://www.bbc.co.uk/history/ancient/romans/tech_01.shtml
BBC site that asks 'What did the Romans ever do for us?'

http://www.historyforkids.org/learn/romans/architecture/romarch.htm
History for Kids page with links about Roman architecture.

INDEX